Original title:
Beneath the Tree Line

Copyright © 2025 Creative Arts Management OÜ
All rights reserved.

Author: Dorian Ashford
ISBN HARDBACK: 978-1-80567-332-3
ISBN PAPERBACK: 978-1-80567-631-7

The Sylvan Silence

In the woods where squirrels play,
A raccoon snatched my sandwich away!
With acorns falling like little bombs,
Nature's chaos has its charms.

The owl hoots out a wise old joke,
While rabbits giggle, all hearts bespoke.
A deer in shades of velvet bright,
Winks at me, 'Let's party tonight!'

Where Roots Embrace the Earth

Roots twist and tangle, a messy hairdo,
Trying to pull off a look that's brand new.
'Look at me!' shouts a sprightly vine,
'I'm the trendsetter of this forest line!'

The mushrooms giggle in polka-dot fun,
'We're the celebrities, on the run!
With a dance move that would make you cheer,
They leap and twirl, then disappear.

Murmurs of Moss and Fern

Moss whispers secrets, soft and low,
'Care for a laugh? I'm in the know!'
Ferns sway gently, a dance so grand,
'We'll put on a show, just give us a hand!'

A beetle stumbles, a comical fall,
The trees all chuckle, 'Did you see that sprawl?'
With twinkling rays the sun does beam,
Nature's a stage, or so it would seem!

A Tapestry of Leaves

Leaves rustle softly, a whispered cheer,
'Who wore it best?' they giggle near.
Red, yellow, and green in a wild spree,
Fashion week in the forest, can you see?

The wind plays tag, a game of chase,
Spinning round in a leafy embrace.
While grumpy old branches shake their head,
'Young folks these days—leave them for dead!'

Hushed Conversations of Leaves

In the rustle of whispers, they plot and play,
Squirrels eavesdrop, while branches sway.
"I swear they saw me steal that nut!"
A hearty laugh echoes, the chatter won't shut.

Sunlight dances, casting shadowy jokes,
While ants march in line, like little folks.
"Is this a parade, or a snack run gone wrong?"
Giggles ensue, as they hum nature's song.

Canopy Dreams

High above, a cloud floats past with glee,
"Is this a dream or just lunch for a bee?"
Branches sway to a rhythm quite sweet,
While owls debate who gets the next meet.

The sun pokes through in a mischievous way,
Sprinkling laughter on all at play.
"Why do trees never play hide and seek?"
"Because they always stand tall, and their roots are meek!"

Under the Verdant Sky

A chameleon smiles, blending with glee,
"Are we hiding, or just too slow for the bee?"
Frogs bounce like jesters, full of delight,
While crickets chirp jokes that stretch through the night.

Fungi laugh low, in a mossy design,
"Did you hear that one about losing your spine?"
Laughter erupts from the bugs and the dew,
Nature's own comedy club, always anew!

Roots that Bind

Tangled together in a playful embrace,
"My roots are your roots, what a silly case!"
A vine winks, sharing gossip galore,
"Did you hear about the tree that thought it could soar?"

Mushrooms tease as they pop up with flair,
"Who needs a chair when you've got a fresh layer?"
Burrowing beetles chuckle and grin,
Binding their stories, where all fun begins.

Beneath the Arching Boughs

Squirrels conspire with acorn schemes,
While birds chatter of nutty dreams.
The sun peeks through a leafy veil,
As laughter rides on the breezy sail.

A raccoon rummages for a midnight snack,
His bandit mask makes him look quite whack.
The trees giggle with each rustling tune,
With shadows dancing beneath the moon.

Remnants of the Forest Floor

Mushrooms sprout like silly hats,
While snails race slowly—what acrobats!
Leaves crunch under every little foot,
Each step taken with a playful hoot.

A fox prances by with a funny stance,
Poking fun at a grasshopper's dance.
The ground is a stage for critter shows,
With laughter hidden where no one goes.

Stories of the Sylvan Realm

Trees whisper secrets of days gone by,
Of owls that hoot and squirrels that fly.
Every rustle tells a comical tale,
Of trolls getting stuck in a stinky pail.

A deer trips over roots in disgrace,
While a rabbit giggles, laughing in place.
These tales weave through branches and leaves,
With humor that even the oak tree believes.

Twilight in the Thicket

The sun dips low, the stars start to yawn,
Bats zoom around like tiny drawn.
The mood is set for a jolly fright,
With critters planning a spooky night.

A hedgehog dons a goofy disguise,
While fireflies twinkle like mischievous eyes.
In the dusk, the woods come alive,
With funny creatures ready to thrive.

Beneath the Foliage's Embrace

Squirrels debate over acorn wealth,
While rabbits gossip, forget their health.
A fox in a bow tie, quite the sight,
Claims he'll dance with owls every night.

Nature's council, in a leafy hall,
Debates who's friendliest, answers small.
The trees all nod, their branches sway,
As chipmunks vote for a nutty buffet.

Conversations with the Wind

The breeze tickles leaves, whispers of fun,
"Did you see that raccoon? He danced as I spun!"
A gust says, "Hold on, I've got to confess,
The deer's fashion sense? I must say, no less!"

They giggle and swirl, causing branches to sway,
Two birds chirp, "Let's play hide and seek today!"
With each fluttering leaf, secrets unfurl,
As critters invent their own chaotic world.

The Stillness of the Green

Amidst the calm, a tortoise sprawls wide,
Declares, "I'm the king, I've nothing to hide!"
While the grasshopper leaps, with a comedic flair,
"Your crown seems too heavy, you're stuck in your chair!"

The daisies chuckle, sharing their views,
On fashion trends known by the woodland hues.
A bear in a hammock snores loud like a truck,
Dreams of a picnic, but fears he's out of luck.

Under the Woodland Whisper

The trees start to gossip, with rustles and creaks,
"Did you hear the moose's new pair of sneaks?"
A squirrel retorts, "Well, I've heard it said,
That he dances at night, but trips on his head!"

Mushrooms giggle, "We can't let it slide,
He still thinks he's smooth, with a goofy stride!"
A twig snaps, laughter soars up to the sky,
As the forest unites in a playful sigh.

The Hidden World Above

Squirrels in tuxedos dance and prance,
Chasing acorns in a nutty romance.
Birds wearing hats sing songs so sweet,
While owls roll their eyes at the foolish beat.

A raccoon with shades gives a cheeky grin,
As he dives for a snack he's planning to win.
Branches sway like a festive parade,
In this wild, leafy masquerade.

Beneath the Boughs

Frogs play leapfrog for a grand old prize,
While bugs in tuxes try to impress flies.
A turtle in flip-flops takes a slow stroll,
Claiming he's faster, just playing a role.

A hedgehog in shades orders drinks at the bar,
Sipping a smoothie, looking like a star.
The breeze giggles softly, tickling the grass,
As every critter waits for the fun to amass.

Twilight Under the Thicket

At dusk, the shadows come out to play,
With fireflies twinkling, leading the way.
A dancing raccoon steals everyone's snacks,
While a bashful possum just nervously cracks.

The rabbits compete in a wacky race,
With carrots as trophies they eagerly chase.
Then frogs start a band with percussion and croaks,
Creating a symphony of silliness and jokes.

Secrets of the Understory

In the underbrush, a party awaits,
Where mushrooms wear hats and dance in pairs.
Fireflies are DJs, spinning lights with glee,
While worms create fashion, trendy as can be.

Snails in a marathon take their sweet time,
Declaring their speed is simply sublime.
This hidden realm bustles, filled to the brim,
With laughter and color, on a whimsical whim.

The Enchanted Glade

There's a squirrel with a stash of more nuts,
He thinks he's a king, and we're just his cups.
His throne is a branch, a great leafy seat,
And he yells at the birds, "You can't have my treat!"

The mushrooms are wearing their best little hats,
While rabbits hold dances, inviting the cats.
The frogs croak in tune, with a beat they contain,
And butterflies giggle as they flutter in vain.

A chipmunk chases shadows, thinks he's quite sly,
Until he trips over, oh my, oh my!
He tumbles and rolls to the base of a fir,
And sighs, "I'm not clumsy; I'm practicing stir!"

With laughter and mischief, the glade comes alive,
Where critters make jokes that only they thrive.
If you find this odd, well, just take a seat,
You'll chuckle when nature spins tales of the sweet.

Serenade of the Glens

In the depths of the glens where the shadows play tricks,
The otters are juggling, performing cool kicks.
The fairies are laughing, their giggles like bells,
As they spill tiny secrets that nobody tells.

The hedgehogs did form a waltzing parade,
Whilst the owls took a break from their nightly crusade.
They hoot in confusion, with spectacles lost,
As the fireflies dart 'round, a glowing exhaust.

A bear in a bow tie just waltzed by a tree,
Claiming, "I'm dapper! Oh, can't you all see?"
The bees are the band, with a buzz and a sting,
As the blossoms all sway, they are singing their fling.

With whispers of mischief, the glens hum a tune,
A symphony blares under the light of the moon.
If you hear laughter echo, don't take it too hard,
It's just nature's own concert, performed in the yard.

Nature's Hidden Sanctuaries

In nooks of the wild, where the clovers are sweet,
Lies a party of crickets, with rhythm in beat.
They chirp out the stories, of days filled with glee,
While ants do the tango, all under a tree.

The badgers discuss all the gossip in town,
While the hedgehogs spin tales that will turn you around.
A fox wears a monocle, claims he's refined,
And the doves roll their eyes, but they're too sweet to mind.

A snail slides on stage in a swanky new shell,
Claiming, "I'm fast! Watch me, won't you dwell?"
The frogs join the chorus with croaks loud and proud,
As the sun dips low, amidst laughter, they crowd.

Hidden treasures of laughter, the sanctuaries hold,
With nature's own humor in stories retold.
So tiptoe through these woods, where the whimsies run free,
And join in the fun, oh, how merry will be!

Footfalls in the Forest

With footfalls in forests where shadows entwine,
The squirrels do gossip on leaves and on pine.
They chat about humans, how funny they seem,
With their clumsy big boots and their coffee supreme.

Under foliage thick, where the tall whispers roam,
The deer play charades, thinking they're home.
A bear tries to dance, but he's got two left feet,
Yet he joins in the fun, with a slip and a beat.

The rabbits are scheming, with wild little grins,
They bet on the turtles for racing, who wins?
And the owls hoot softly, with wisecracks galore,
While the trees listen close, just waiting for more.

So wander these trails where the footfalls do speak,
In the forest's embrace, find the humor unique.
For each leaf and each twig has a story to tell,
That laughter echoes softly, all under nature's spell.

The Realm of Starlit Leaves

In a world of leafy giggles,
Squirrels plot their acorn heists,
Whispers of the rustling treetops,
Echo jokes that nature writes.

The moonlight winks through branches,
As rabbits tell their hare-raising tales,
While owls hoot with knowing chuckles,
And the wind's laughter sails.

Mice dance in the silver shadows,
Their tiny feet click on the ground,
Foxes grin at the antics,
As mischief whirls all around.

Underneath the comical canopy,
Life thrives in a playful spree,
With every rustle and flutter,
The woods burst with jollity.

The Forest's Heartbeat

The trees giggle, their branches sway,
As chipmunks juggle nuts all day,
Beneath the boughs, the laughter grows,
Where even the shyest critter shows.

A bear trips over roots it knows,
While foxes play tic-tac-toe in rows,
Each frog croaks with a splashy cheer,
Nature's humor sounds crystal clear.

With crickets playing tiny drums,
And fireflies brightly buzzing hums,
Woodpeckers drum a funky beat,
As the forest dances to its own sweet treat.

In this realm where life unfolds,
Funny tales and laughter mold,
With every rustle, every bark,
A joyful symphony in the dark.

Under the Arching Branches

In a nook where the shadows prance,
Birds throw a winged dance,
Silly squirrels from limb to limb,
Crafting acrobatics on a whim.

Bushes chuckle, flowers grin,
As bees are buzzing with a spin,
Rabbits in a hopping race,
Chasing dreams in nature's space.

A porcupine trips, spikes askew,
While ants march in a parade, too,
Even the snails wear silly hats,
Their tiny laughter filling like chats.

Gathered fruits sway in jest,
As playful winds give them rest,
The canopy holds secrets cherished,
With joy in nature, we're all nourished.

An Ode to the Shadows

Oh shadows that dance in twilight glow,
Holding secrets we want to know,
The giggling leaves in the evening breeze,
Invite us to join them, if you please.

A lazy raccoon, with a sly grin,
Steals snacks from the picnic bin,
While owls wink with a knowing eye,
Spreading laughter as they fly by.

Was that a bear in a tutu spun?
Or just a trickster playing for fun?
As light fades and giggles cross,
The woods hold tales, not a loss.

So here's to the laughter in shadowed glades,
A whimsical place where joy cascades,
In the heart of nature, let's make a pact,
To chase the funny moments, that's a fact!

Reverie in the Grove

In a grove where shadows play,
Squirrel steals my snack away.
Branches sway, the breeze lets slip,
   A bird sings, a fuzzy quip.

Laughter echoes, there's a gaffe,
Woodpecker's gone and made me laugh.
Nature's charms, a jester's flair,
With every rustle, whispers dare.

Acorns drop, a little thud,
Plunked upon my hat, oh crud!
The squirrel grins, I've lost my seat,
   A toppled branch—what a feat!

Beneath the green, the antics grow,
With every turn, there's more to show.
Giggling leaves and giggler's tales,
Life's a romp where laughter trails.

Canopy Dreams

Up above, a riddle spun,
Where does the sun hide from fun?
Twinkle toes of light take flight,
While squirrels debate day and night.

Raccoons in suits, plotting a scheme,
Tipping their hats, in a moonbeam.
Beneath the leaves, their laughter swells,
A cacophony of furry bells.

Chasing shadows, what a race,
Fallen leaves are the new base.
A sliding contest down the bark,
Squeaks and giggles as they embark.

In a bower where whimsy thrives,
The canopy gnaws, and joy derives.
Tails entwined in playful strife,
In this forest, giggles are life!

The Dance of Dappled Light

Flickering shadows, a jig begins,
Leaves chuckle softly as daylight spins.
In beams of joy, a salsa plays,
While the glowworms prance in tangled ways.

Mossy carpets, where the rabbits glide,
In twirls and leaps, they hope to hide.
A hiccup here, a tumble there,
Nature's orchestra of joyful flair.

Prancing fawns with awkward grace,
Wobbling around in unexpected space.
Sunbeams tap dance on their backs,
With every sway, the forest cracks.

Every leaf a giggly wink,
Life's a sketch, more fun than you think.
In the light, they sway and sway,
Join the fun—come laugh and play!

Ferns and Folklore

Ferns in the corner, whisper tales,
Of mischievous elves and fairy trails.
A snicker shared among soft fronds,
Secrets linger like gentle ponds.

Each twig a clue, a riddle to solve,
Knotted roots in curious evolve.
Gnomes pop up for a chat or jest,
With every word, they love their quest.

Bouncing mushrooms wear silly hats,
While toads sit by, sharing cute spats.
In laughter lost through the bramble thick,
A chorus of chuckles, nature's trick.

So gather 'round for a woodland tale,
Where ferns and laughter set the sail.
In the quiet, mischief calls,
With silly stories in the woodlands' halls.

Dance of the Wildflowers

In the meadow, blooms sway,
Dancing like they're at a ball.
Flowers gossip in bright display,
Whispering secrets, sharing all.

Bees with tuxedos, buzzing loud,
Are the bouncers of this dance.
Pollen confetti falling proud,
Clover starts its funny prance.

Ladybugs wearing polka dots,
Join the jive with little spins.
Their tiny moves can't be forgot,
As nature's laughter sweetly wins.

So take a step in grassy cheer,
Join the chorus, wiggle too!
Nature's party, loud and clear,
Under the sun, just me and you.

Lullabies of the Undergrowth

In the bushes, critters hum,
A lullaby that makes me smile.
Crickets chirp a steady drum,
While slumber creeps with style.

A raccoon yawns, stretches wide,
His antics never end with grace.
He thinks he's smooth, but oh, he's tried,
To sneak a snack, it's quite the chase!

A hedgehog snoozes, curled in tight,
Dreaming of snacks and midnight feasts.
Squirrels join in, oh what a sight,
Stealing dreams of nuts, the little beasts!

So let the whispers guide your mind,
With nature's lullaby around.
In this cozy world, unwind,
Where chuckles and peace can be found.

Traces of the Timberland

Among the trunks, the stories roam,
A raccoon's trail, a squirrel's race.
Nature's mischief finds a home,
In every bark, there's a playful trace.

Woodpeckers tap a funky beat,
Like drummers in a forest jam.
They keep it cool, stay on their feet,
Playing tunes like a woodland band.

Fungi pop up, all shapes and sizes,
Playing hide and seek by the path.
Their colors tease, their odd disguises,
Adding humor to nature's math.

So wander through this leafy stage,
Where every nook holds a surprise.
With every step, you turn the page,
Of funny tales beneath the skies.

Moments Under the Foliage

Under the leaves, a giggle grows,
A little snail claims the best seat.
He's quite the show, as everyone knows,
In this shady, leafy retreat.

Mice in sneakers race with delight,
And frogs leap in a silly contest.
Jumping high with all their might,
Nature's laughs are truly the best.

Chipmunks scurry with acorn stacks,
As if they're prepping for a feast.
Who knew these woods were full of acts?
An endless show, to say the least!

So grab a snack, take a seat,
Join the fun, don't be shy.
Every moment here is a treat,
As nature winks and passes by.

The Language of Old Growth

The ancient tree stands tall and wise,
With knots and rings like secrets in disguise.
Whispers of squirrels dance in the breeze,
While owls share gossip, if you please.

Roots tangled like stories, old and thick,
A beetle's request? "Please, just one stick!"
Branches overhead, a stage for the show,
The sloth performs, moving way too slow!

Bees buzz like chatter, they're buzzing with cheer,
While raccoons plot mischief with mischievous sneer.
A woodpecker drums, conducting the tune,
As a hare hops by, shouting, "Dude, that's a moon!"

Leaves sip the sun like it's herbal tea,
While branches debate if they should be free.
The dance of the forest, chaotic and bright,
A comedy special, beneath the moonlight.

Hidden Paths of the Wilderness

In the wild where the maps often fail,
A fox claims the trail, leaving a tail.
"I know a shortcut," he brags with a grin,
Climbing over logs, what a dubious win!

A deer tells his jokes, well-practiced and clear,
While ducks throw shade with mischievous cheer.
The path only twists where the mushrooms grow,
And a rabbit keeps watch, critiquing the show.

Amid the green thickets, with flowers so bright,
A porcupine ponders, "Is that moon really white?"
But skunks roll their eyes, "It's just a big glow,
Trust me, I've checked. It's not like you know!"

The trees gossip loudly, each branch has a say,
While butterflies flit, like, "Join our ballet!"
In the hidden paths, where no one would stare,
The wilderness laughs, with the world unaware!

Whispers in the Bark

On a bark where the ants hold up their parade,
Each groove tells a tale, some sweet and some fayed.
"What do you call a tree that's too loud?"
It jokes with the woodpecker, "Way too proud!"

Insects confide, "This bark is our home,
With real estate value? Just don't roam!"
A caterpillar giggles, "Look, I'm a snack!"
While spiders just sigh, tying up a whole pack.

And the moss spreads rumors, thick on the floor,
"They think they're the best, but who keeps the score?"
A wise old owl hoots, "Let's keep it real,
Who's got the best 'tweet', is the ultimate deal!"

Layers of laughter, woven and spread,
Each crack in the bark, where the giggles are fed.
The trees sway to secrets, in rhythm and rhyme,
With the nature of comedy, standing the test of time.

Symphony of the Seasons

Winter arrives in a snowy white coat,
While squirrels in mittens plan how to gloat.
"Did you see my stash?" one says with a grin,
But summer's a party they stole from within!

Spring flings around blooms, all fresh and so bright,
With tulips that chatter, debating the height.
As the wind plays the flute, the crickets then join,
In a summer jam session—oh, pure joy!

Autumn struts in with a bold, rustling flair,
The leaves throw confetti without a care.
"Why are we falling?" they giggle and sway,
While the wind calls the shots, making them play!

Each season a chapter, a messy old book,
Nature's great playhouse, where all are off-hook.
And in the vast theater, the forest agrees,
It's a comical show, filled with giggles and trees!

Echoes in the Shade

In the woods I hear a sound,
A squirrel with nuts he's found.
He drops one, then looks around,
So much for being keen and proud.

A rabbit hops, oh what a sight,
Dancing like he's full of flight.
He trips on roots, what a delight,
Now he's rolling left and right!

The old owl hoots with glee,
Says he's wiser than the sea.
But even he gets stuck in trees,
Who's the wise one? Not he!

The shadows laugh, they play a game,
Hide and seek is such a fame.
In this world, we all exclaim,
Life is funny, not just plain.

Shadows of the Timbers

A bear in a hat? Oh, what a scene,
He thinks he's suave, a sight unseen.
He trips on vines, falls in between,
Muffin crumbs are his cuisine!

The foxes gossip, tails entwined,
Predicting where the next snack's reclined.
But one gets caught, now how unkind,
In a trap of twigs, totally maligned!

A turtle races at a slow pace,
Underestimating the forest's grace.
He calls it a marathon, what a face,
Victory? Not, that's the case!

Chirping birds make funny tunes,
Singing love songs to the moons.
But they sound like clowns with big balloons,
Oh how we laugh, and that's just June!

Underneath the Green Veil

In a shady nook, I see a prank,
A raccoon steals food, quite the tank.
He nibbles on chips, what a flank,
While folks just stare, mouths agank!

The trees whisper jokes, quite absurd,
One says, "Knock, knock," with a bird.
It's a riot, just look at the herd,
Who knew nature could be so stirred!

A moose struts by, stylishly late,
He thinks he's the king; what a fate!
But ducks all quack, they celebrate,
"King of the woods? It's first-rate!"

With laughter shared, the forest thrives,
Silly antics come alive.
In this green hall where fun derives,
Life's a joke, but oh, we strive!

Grace of the Woodland Realm

In the woodland realm, mischief abounds,
Chipmunks race, they're wearing crowns.
They squeak and squeal with chipper sounds,
Who knew such silliness was found?

A lizard slips on morning dew,
He slides right past a cat that's blue.
"Oh dear!" the lizard squeaks anew,
Impromptu gymnastics, who knew?

Mice hold a party, balloons in tow,
Dancing round as they steal the show.
But oops! The cheese, they overthrow,
And chaos reigns, it's quite the low!

Nature's circus, oh what a thrill,
Each critter plays a quirky skill.
With laughter swirling, it's such a fill,
In these woods, joy's the perfect will.

Echoes of Rustic Life

In the shade of branches wide,
The squirrels dance with utmost pride.
They chatter loud, a raucous choir,
While I sip tea by the campfire.

A raccoon steals my sandwich bright,
With a look that's pure delight.
He winks, then scurries up the tree,
Ah, dinner guest? Just not for me!

The frogs jump in a leaping race,
A championship in this green space.
Their croaks are scores, a symphony,
Of nature's own cacophony.

The ants march by, with tiny feet,
On search for crumbs, their tasty treat.
I laugh at them, such busy bees,
In a world where not much can tease!

Harmonies of Hidden Trails

Through twisted paths our laughter flows,
Where every twist brings silly woes.
The bushes rustle, a prankster's call,
As we trip and stumble, just about to fall.

A deer peeks out with curious eyes,
As if to judge our slapstick tries.
It snickers soft, in woodland's glee,
'What a show, just let me be!'

With each step, the snacks we bring,
Are half-eaten, and pranks take wing.
A hidden stash of gumdrops sweet,
Now bounces 'round on tiny feet.

At dusk we find our way back home,
With branches tangled in my comb.
The echo of laughter trails behind,
In this green world, oh so kind!

Interludes in the Green

Where ferns unfurl in sunlight's beam,
And carrots plot an underground scheme.
The tomatoes gossip from their vine,
About the radish who crossed the line.

Bumblebees buzz with comic flair,
Dancing like they don't have a care.
While butterflies flaunt their fashion show,
In colors that steal the very show!

The picnic's set, but ants invade,
A marching band of silly brigade.
They steal my cheese—it's quite absurd,
In this ballet, I'm just a blurred word.

And as we feast in this absurd plot,
With nature's whimsy, we're quite the lot.
In the green, the laughs blend and twirl,
A circus floor, with a twinkling swirl!

Nature's Hidden Chamber

In the grove where secrets grow,
Laughter echoes, tales to sow.
A gopher's peek, a squirrel's delight,
Their jokes fly high, oh what a sight!

Beneath the leaves, a mushroom groans,
With jokes only the toads have known.
They chuckle deep, in timeless glee,
While I ponder if life's just a spree.

With every rustle, a chuckle rings,
As nature tries on her silly things.
A feathered friend mimics a snore,
I can't help but laugh, wanting more!

And as the sun dips low for the night,
The fireflies join in—what a sight!
With tiny lights and playful sway,
In this hidden chamber, we laugh and play!

Nature's Gentle Mantle

In the woods where squirrels dance,
A raccoon steals a glance,
Chasing shadows in the sun,
Nature's game has just begun.

Birds squawk in a playful fight,
Over breadcrumbs, what a sight!
I trip on roots and laugh aloud,
As a deer stares, quite proud.

The sunbeams tickle the ground,
Where mischief in the air is found,
A fox prances with such flair,
Wearing leaves like a hat, I swear!

The breeze whispers a giggling tune,
As ants march in a wild platoon,
Laughter echoes through the trees,
Nature's joke? A buzzing bee!

The Song of Silent Steps

With every step, a stick does crack,
Nature chuckles at my knack,
The path is full of twisty trails,
Where bushes hide all sorts of gales.

A turtle lags, but has no rush,
I scramble past in a mad dash hush,
Frogs leap up with a loud 'ribbit,'
While I pretzel-step, oh the limit!

The shadows tease my wandering feet,
As I chase a squirrel down the street,
It stops to giggle, then it chews,
I laugh, for I've lost my shoes!

Each twig I snap, a tune is born,
Nature's joke is never worn,
With every silent step I take,
I trip on leaves, my ankles ache!

The Lullaby of Leaves

Leaves rustle like a playful muse,
Whispering secrets, sharing news,
A chipmunk winks, a gentle tease,
As I try to climb, but slip with ease.

A breeze blows softly, like a sigh,
I wave at clouds that drift on by,
While out of nowhere, a raindrop plops,
Nature's chance to catch my hops!

The sun dips low, it paints the floor,
A canvas where I stumble more,
A squirrel chortles at my plight,
As I dance with shadows, oh what a sight!

The evening brings a soft embrace,
As I trip and fall in the mossy space,
But laughter rings where calm does weave,
In the lullaby of leaves, I believe!

Reflections in the Forest's Mirror

In a pond that shows my shocked face,
I stare at ducks that waddle at pace,
The water ripples with each silly grin,
While I ponder the depth of my chin.

Trees stand tall with a knowing smile,
As I trip around, it takes a while,
A butterfly lands and gives me a tease,
Bidding me to dance with the trees.

Mirror, mirror, on the ground,
Where frogs leap and my laughter's found,
A selfie with a crab who grins wide,
In nature's mirror, I can't hide!

With each step, the forest laughs,
While I chase shadows and examine paths,
The joy in each reflection shines,
As I embrace these forest lines!

Twilight's Gentle Touch

In the hush of dusk, the critters play,
Chasing shadows that dance and sway.
A squirrel dropped acorns from way too high,
While a raccoon just waved his paws goodbye.

The owl hooted jokes, but no one could hear,
As the fireflies flickered, casting cheer.
A rabbit in glasses read a map,
Got lost in the pages, fell into a trap.

A deer took a selfie, with a grin so wide,
While a hedgehog rolled by, on an unsteady ride.
Laughter echoed, if trees could chuckle,
In this paradise, worries begin to shuffle.

So gather your friends for a twilight spree,
Where laughter and mirth reign wild and free.
For under the soft dusk's merry embrace,
Nature's comedians put on a grand showcase.

Life Under the Leafy Veil

In leafy realms, life's a circus act,
With raccoons in capes, that's a solid fact.
The bushes all whisper their comical tales,
Where chipmunks are kings with their tiny scale.

A snail in a shell said, "Catch me, if you dare!"
But he always got stuck, in his own despair.
The ferns just laughed, with their feathery fronds,
As dandelions danced like fluffy blondes.

A bear tried to skateboard, lost his cool,
While the frogs croaked hymns by a makeshift pool.
A turtle debated, "Am I slow by choice?"
"Or just more relaxed?" he pondered, with poise.

So come join the throng, and witness this play,
Nature's comedy show is here to stay.
Under the leafy canopy's gentle embrace,
You'll find the world is a whimsical place.

The Veil of Verdant Thorns

In a patch of green where giggles arise,
A bushy old hedgehog wears mismatched ties.
A porcupine strutted, but pricked his own shoe,
"Fashion's a gamble, but I'm feeling brand new!"

The thorns gave a nod, they were quite the crew,
While butterflies chuckled, "What's wrong with you?"
An ant with a backpack trekked on with glee,
Singing songs of picnic plans, just you wait and see.

A lizard performed with a hat on his head,
He juggled sweet berries, a feast to be fed.
But one fell and splattered, making all squeal,
The roars of laughter were hard to conceal.

So venture this way for a laugh-filled spree,
With mishaps and fun 'neath the canopy tree.
In the realm of thorns, where humor takes flight,
Nature whispers jokes beneath the soft night.

Enchanted by the Woodlands

In the heart of the woods, mischief takes flight,
Where the squirrels hold court from morning to night.
A fox in a tuxedo, with grace and a jig,
Proclaimed he's the best dancer—much to the pig.

A raccoon named Rocky, with tales so tall,
Tried fishing with marshmallows, didn't catch a thing at all.
The rabbits giggled, hiding their grins,
While a beaver hosted games with toothy big wins.

The trees wore their leaves like a fashionable cape,
As the critters all gathered, no need for escape.
A turtle in shades said, "I'm the cool one here!"
With laughter resounding, there was nothing to fear.

So wander this way, let the antics unfold,
Where tales of the woodlands are timelessly told.
With heart and with humor, we'll dance through the glade,
In a world of pure wonder, foundations we've laid.

Where the Wild Things Retreat

In leafy dens where creatures hide,
The wild things frolic, full of pride.
They dance around in furry suits,
Swapping tales of funny loots.

A wise old owl with glasses perched,
Reads bedtime stories, a laugh unearthed.
Squirrels chuckle at their grand parade,
While raccoons plan a nutty escapade.

Goat voices echo, 'What's for lunch?'
A porcupine says, 'My thorns? A crunch!'
The laughter rolls like gentle streams,
In this forest where humor beams.

At day's end, they gather round,
To share the funniest things they've found.
Beneath the branchy, happy spree,
Are lines of laughter, wild and free.

Secrets Cradled in Rooted Shadows

Where shadows dwell and secrets play,
The gnomes tell jokes that fly away.
A rabbit bursts with giggles bright,
While turtles race, yet lose their sight.

'Am I too slow?' the turtle sighs,
'To beat that rabbit? Oh, what lies!'
The grass whispers with giggles low,
As mushrooms join the silly show.

A hedgehog claims he's quite the chef,
'With acorn stew, you'll laugh 'til breath!'
But elderly bugs just roll their eyes,
Saying, 'Mayhaps next time, aim for pies.'

Rooted secrets in laughter found,
Tickle the earth, they twist around.
For in their shade, the fun runs free,
In whispers and murmurs beneath the spree.

The Symphony of Shelter

In branches high, a concert plays,
Where critters gather, dance all day.
The chirps and beeps create a tune,
As raccoons sway beneath the moon.

A squirrel conducts with tiny paws,
Mastering all of nature's laws.
Beetles play the drums with flair,
As fireflies light the rhythm in air.

The fox sings bass in shadows deep,
While owls provide a peaceful peep.
Their melodies lift the spirits high,
Floating above like clouds in the sky.

But suddenly a cat sneezes loud,
The concert halts, all creatures bowed.
Yet laughter breaks where music thrived,
And under the stars, their joy survived.

Earth's Embrace

In cozy nooks, the laughter swells,
As critters share their slip and fells.
A mole once tried to dance on air,
But ended up with dirt to spare.

The winds carry tales of silly fights,
Between the ants on candy nights.
They march to claim their treasure trove,
Yet stumble over, as spirits rove.

'Your sandwiches are just for show!'
A bee tells a mouse with a grand 'Hello!'
And underneath the leafy tide,
The earth holds secrets, laughter wide.

In this embrace, with joy we roam,
A woodland space, we call our home.
For in the heart of nature's grace,
Are giggles shared in sacred space.

The Stories Nestled Amongst the Roots

A squirrel claimed a treasure chest,
With acorns stacked like silly jest.
The tales it told of daring feats,
Had us all in laughing fits.

A rabbit's hat began to twitch,
As magic made the flowers itch.
From left to right, they danced and spun,
In a comical race to greet the sun.

The fox was dressed in fancy shoes,
It boasted tricks and clever clues.
But tripped on roots, did faceplant wrong,
And thus became the punchline song.

The mushrooms giggled in delight,
As critters swapped their hats each night.
From rambunctious tales to whispered lore,
Each root holds laughter, evermore.

In the Shelter of Shade

Under patches of leafy cover,
A frog sang songs with pop and hover.
His voice did croak, a laughable show,
As flies took turns in a humorous flow.

A bear tried to nap, but bees had their game,
They buzzed and tickled, he could not tame.
With flailing paws and grumpy frowns,
He stumbled into the jester towns.

The shadows danced with every gust,
Even the stones began to rust.
In this haven where humor breeds,
Nature's fun is all that it needs.

A picnic spread was what they sought,
But ants arrived—oh, twist of thought!
With goofy moves and stolen bites,
The critters feasted on silly nights.

The Magic Within the Greenery

A potion brewed in a teacup small,
Resulted in hiccups, the silliest call.
The grasshoppers joined in a wobbly jig,
As magic spread like a fuzzy twig.

A firefly burst with laughter bright,
While fluttering near—such a wondrous sight!
They swapped their glows like fashion treats,
Creating chaos in summer's heats.

In the thicket, a dance with sticks,
The rabbits twirled in playful tricks.
With leafy hats and flowered ties,
From every nook, laughter could rise.

A sage old owl observed the fun,
In cloaks of shadows, he spun and spun.
He muttered tales of whimsical glee,
In the heart of nature's jubilee.

Stillness Among the Bark

The logs would whisper in quiet tones,
Telling tales to the wandering stones.
A snail crept slow, with grand ideas,
That tickled the roots and brought out cheers.

A blink of an eye, the woodpecker danced,
A tap-tap-tap as the creatures pranced.
Yet slipped on sap with a comic splat,
He turned to grin, as proud as a cat.

The wind blew softly, with secrets aplenty,
As laughter soared, and worries grew lightly.
In the cocoon of bark and fate,
A funny whisper kept thinking straight.

With each passing leaf, new humor grew,
From every nook, a jest to pursue.
In stillness, a comedy we find,
The branches hold joy, intertwined.

Whispers of the Canopy

Squirrels speak in secret codes,
Telling tales of acorn roads.
They plot their next great nutty scheme,
While insects dance, a tiny dream.

A woodpecker knocks on tree trunk walls,
Declaring it the loudest of calls.
The rabbits giggle, rolling around,
As leaves keep falling without a sound.

Caterpillars wear their pajamas bright,
Convinced they'll fly by morning light.
Yet none have told them of the fate,
Of butterflies who just can't wait.

The sun sneaks through in playful rays,
Illuminating silly ways.
From branch to branch, the laughter flows,
In this lush realm, where fun just grows.

Shadows Among the Branches

In the shade where shadows creep,
A raccoon takes a snooze, deep.
He dreams of pizza, what a sight,
As he dribbles drool in the dim twilight.

Frogs perform a midnight show,
Croaking tunes with jazzy flow.
A firefly flashes like a star,
Swearing it will become a star car.

Hedgehogs drag their spiky spines,
Wearing hats made of thick vines.
They hold a party, no invite,
With snacks of mushrooms, oh what a bite!

The shadows laugh, the moon peeks through,
With winks and glimmers, it joins the crew.
In this odd world, where all is free,
Every creature grins with glee.

Secrets of the Woodland

The owls hoot with wisdom wise,
But secretly plot their surprise.
For every mouse who dares to peek,
They throw a party, oh so unique!

Little mice in fanciful hats,
Dancing with frogs, and friendly bats.
They spin and twirl on tiny toes,
In the woods where mischief flows.

A badger juggles acorns high,
As the rabbits cheer, oh my, oh my!
With every drop, they all just laugh,
For fun is easy when it's on the path.

The trees sway gently, watching the fun,
Rooted in joy for everyone.
In this woodland, secrets are shared,
For laughter blooms where no one's scared.

Echoes from the Underbrush

In the underbrush, a giggle escapes,
Sprinkling joy like silly shapes.
A hedgehog rolls, a tumble spins,
As birds drop pebbles, oh what a win!

Chirps and chirrups fill the air,
As bushy-tailed friends declare,
"Who's the fastest across the glade?"
"Me!" shouts the turtle, unafraid.

With blooms of color, they clash and cheer,
The chattering crickets lend an ear.
A parade of creatures, prancing about,
With a bark of laughter, they twist and shout.

The thicket hums a song of delight,
For every rustle hides a spark of light.
Echoes bounce in a funny dance,
In this wild world, we all take a chance.

Nestled in Nature's Arms

In a cozy nook where the critters dwell,
A squirrel once thought he knew it well.
But every leaf that rustled near,
He thought was a bear, and let out a cheer!

A raccoon waddled, his belly quite round,
While chipmunks scolded from nearby ground.
They laughed and danced in a merry whirl,
As nature's song became a silly twirl.

The owls hooted with comic sync,
While frogs croaked jokes that made you think.
Between the trees, they'd take a stand,
As laughter echoed across the land.

So nestle down where the laughter roams,
With furry friends who call this home.
In nature's arms, the joy's a breeze,
Life's a giggle in the shady trees.

A Symphony of Squirrel Calls

A chattering clan in a mighty oak,
Each squirrel with a joke, each joke a poke.
They plan their pranks with squeaky glee,
Launching acorns like they're a jamboree!

One dressed in leaves, another in twine,
Twirling around on a low-hanging vine.
They cackle and chatter, such ruckus they make,
As a breeze gently sways the trunk of the lake.

"Hey! Look at me!" one squirrel declares,
"I can leap and stick like I'm breathing air!"
He fluffs his tail and jumps with style,
Yet lands on his friend, oh what a trial!

Amidst the giggles and playful calls,
Nature's music fills the woods and walls.
In furry chaos, they find their fame,
A symphony of squirrel calls—what a game!

The Forgotten Trail

Once there was a path, hidden from view,
Where lost hikers hoped to find something new.
Yet tangled in brush, it truly did hide,
They stumbled and tumbled, arms open wide!

Piggybacking bugs and a butterfly parade,
The trail became wild; a grand escapade.
"I swear I saw a sign," said one with a frown,
But instead found a mushroom that looked like a crown!

With trees growing over, the path faded slow,
Adventures turned antics, oh where did they go?
A raccoon waved hello with a chuckle and grin,
"Guess you've met the trail that never begins!"

Yet laughter erupted through bushes and brambles,
Their journey became one of whimsical rambles.
In nature's embrace, they danced on this trail,
The forgotten adventure—oh, how they prevail!

Home of the Wandering Shadows

In the twilight hour, shadows dance bold,
A house of whimsy, where stories unfold.
A raccoon playing peekaboo with a starlit grin,
Turned a simple evening into a whimsical spin.

Here a shadow prances, there one takes flight,
Wandering strangers embrace the night.
As owls gossip softly, secrets they keep,
While fireflies twinkle, lighting dreams that leap.

Each nook tells a tale, a giggling plight,
Of playful mischiefs drifting in sight.
Perhaps a lost shoe or a glimmering hat,
The wanderers chuckle at what they have sat.

Home to the shadows, oh what a scene,
A world where the funny meets all that's serene.
Here in the stillness, laughter takes root,
In the dance of the night, there's beauty in pursuit.

Beneath the Drifting Canopy

Squirrels in tuxedos, so dapper and spry,
Hold nuts for a party, oh my, oh my!
They dance on the branches, a wild jubilee,
While birds chirp the tunes, what a sight to see!

A raccoon in sunglasses slides down a tree,
With a snack in his paws, feeling so free.
He invites all his friends for a picnic fun,
But the ants bring the cake and now they're on the run!

In shadows, the laughter of crickets ignites,
As frogs wear top hats and stage silly fights.
The owls roll their eyes at this nonsensical show,
While dawn brings a yawn, as the party's a no-go!

So if you're in need of some mirth and delight,
Just join the tree folks; it's a comedy night!
With nature's own humor, a whimsical spree,
The laughter resounds, come and join in the glee!

Treading the Twilight Trails

A hedgehog in boots struts down a path,
While giggling at shadows, he's bringing the laughs.
He tips his small hat and offers a grin,
As the moon says, 'Hey, let the fun now begin!'

The owls hoot a chorus, their rhythm is grand,
As squirrels throw acorns like they're in a band.
The breeze brings a chuckle, the night's their old pal,
While fireflies flash disco, all the creatures now howl!

Down by the water, the frogs start a fight,
Over who can jump highest under the light.
With splashes and ribbits, they're giving their best,
While turtles just chuckle, thinking, 'What a jest!'

As night starts to wane and the stars dim a bit,
The critters all gather, and they choose to sit.
With dreams of tomorrow, and tales worth a smile,
They rest in the glimmer, it's all been worthwhile!

Glimmers of Forgotten Stories

The ancient tree whispers of times gone by,
With tales of a cat that could jump to the sky.
He'd dog paddle rivers, then leap like a kite,
And boast to the owls of his marvelous flight!

A turtle once claimed he could run like the wind,
While pacing in circles, trying to pretend.
He wore a red cape, oh so chic and so bold,
But the tortoises giggled, 'If only you'd hold!'

An old fox in glasses tells tales of the past,
Of rabbits that danced while they ate their green grass.
He chuckles and winks, for he's seen it all play,
While chipmunks take notes on the zany array!

So gather 'round friends, with a drink and a cheer,
For lessons of laughter, we hold oh so dear.
In tales of the forest, where stories run wild,
We find that the best ones are shared with a smile!

The Woodland's Embrace

In the heart of the forest, a party takes flight,
With mushrooms as tables, and fireflies' light.
They've turned a big log into seating galore,
And all of the bunnies just can't help but roar!

The porcupine bartender, shaking up cheers,
With drinks made of berries, a pint full of sneers.
The deer share a story of their sprinting spree,
While raccoons organize a wild jubilee!

Salamanders juggle, oh what a display,
While owls in tuxedos make rules for the play.
They trade funny quips, their feathers astir,
As the night echoes back with a soft, silly purr!

So come join the revels, and dance 'neath the moon,
With laughter and whimsy, we'll all sing a tune.
In the woodland's embrace, there's joy all around,
Where the humor of nature is truly profound!

The Shade's Embrace

A squirrel with a cap, looking so wise,
Telling tales of nuts, under sunny skies.
The branches giggle, swaying with glee,
As leaves drop like confetti, wild and free.

A shady retreat for a lounging cat,
Who dreams of catching that sneaky rat.
With each lazy stretch, he yawns so wide,
While birds crack jokes, swooping outside.

Beneath the lush green, the earthworms sway,
Dancing to beats of the lively day.
The grass gets tickled by the playful breeze,
It's a funny world with lofty trees!

In the shade's embrace, humor's the key,
For every whimsy is wild and free.
So gather around, leave your worries behind,
In this giggling jungle, hilarity you'll find.

Solace Among the Ferns

Ferns whisper secrets, like teenage teens,
Plotting mischief in emerald greens.
A snail wearing shades, slicker than slick,
Slows down to chat with a wandering stick.

Beneath the fronds where the spiders dance,
A frog croaks sonnets; he took a chance.
His stage a puddle, his audience small,
Yet he sings so loud, it's a laugh for all!

Dancing fireflies are the stars of the night,
With twinkling lights, they take their flight.
They bump into flowers, causing a fuss,
In this leafy realm, there's never a rush!

So take a seat where the laughter rings,
Among the ferns, let your heart take wings.
In nature's comedy, joy's on the page,
So join the troupe, and share the stage!

Secrets of the Bark

Old trees gossip with wrinkles so deep,
While roly-poly bugs giggle and leap.
A rabbit in glasses, reading a tome,
Pretends to be wise, but just wants to roam.

The bark shares tales of the years that flew,
Of frogs on a quest with a magical view.
They ponder the meaning of life and fun,
As ants form a line for their lunch in the sun.

A capricious wind twirls laughter through leaves,
While nature's jesters spin jokes like thieves.
In their realm of whispers, the humor stands tall,
With wit in the roots that connect us all!

Secrets unfold in this silly domain,
Where wisdom's a joke, and silliness reigns.
So listen intently to the stories shared,
For every tree knows, it's never to be spared.

A Breath of Moss

Moss with a smile that's fluffy and light,
Cushions the ground, making all things right.
On its green carpet, a snail takes a nap,
As nearby a beetle plots a mishap.

A bear with a bow tie, quite dapper and spry,
Tries to recite poetry but lets out a sigh.
He's stuck in his thoughts, but can't find a beat,
So he just rolls over, a moose by his feet.

A dandelion's chatter makes the sun laugh out loud,
As butterflies gather, forming a crowd.
In the midst of the laughter, a shadow rolls past,
A turtle excuses himself, moving quite fast!

Here in the layers of green and of gold,
The stories unfold, and the laughter is bold.
So let's take a moment where whimsy does thrive,
In the breath of the moss, we come alive!

Visions Under the Woodland Arch

Squirrels dance in acorn hats,
And rabbits wear their fanciest pants.
The chipmunks hold their secret chats,
While the owls throw their nightly dance.

A raccoon steals a sandwich whole,
While deer critique his taste in bread.
A fox pulls pranks upon the mole,
And giggles while he's safely fled.

The shadows twist, a playful show,
As laughter echoes through the trees.
A waltz of roots with branches low,
It's nature's way of teasing bees.

A bashful gnome is caught in sight,
He trips, falls flat; oh what a mess!
The forest bursts with pure delight,
As trees shake leaves in sheer success.

Tales of the Elder Trees.

Old oaks tell stories of their youth,
They whisper tales of wind and woe.
The pines just laugh and share the truth,
Of squirrels stealing all they know.

A willow weeps, but laughs instead,
For puddles joke with frogs at play.
The birches shake their silver head,
While foxes scheme and hide away.

The maple and the holly feast,
On laughter shared with glowing dusk.
Beware the elf who loves a tease,
For nature's jester plays with musk.

The trees conspire, roots intertwined,
As shadows twirl with moonlight spin.
In every leaf, a joke defined,
The forest grins; we all join in.

Whispers of the Canopy

Up high, the leaves gossip and sway,
While branches giggle without a care.
A hummingbird steals nectar away,
And squirrels dive from midair flair.

The laughter rises with the sun,
As shadows play a peek-a-boo.
"Is that a bear, or just some fun?"
The trees all hush, then laugh anew.

A ladybug spins tales of dare,
While beetles do the limbo pass.
The canopy, a show to share,
Where laughter's light bends blades of grass.

Each rustling leaf, a small delight,
As sunlight paints the forest hue.
In this embrace, the world feels right,
With nature's jesters in full view.

Secrets of the Forest Floor

The mushrooms gather for a chat,
While insects strut in suits of gold.
A hedgehog waltzes; how about that?
And the ants boast tales of treasure untold.

Underneath the frondy bed,
The worms exchange their squirmy tales.
A snail relishes its slow spread,
While dancing with its leafy trails.

A tiny frog hops, full of glee,
Saying, "What's that, a party here?"
The turtle shrugs, "Just come and see,
Dance lightly 'til the dawn draws near!"

Then shadows stretch, and giggles swell,
For secrets shared grow roots of fun.
In every nook, there's laughter's spell,
In this wild realm, joy's never done.

The Canopy's Gentle Watch

In the heights where branches sway,
Squirrels plot their cheeky play,
A raccoon steals a snack from me,
As I sip my herbal tea.

Above my head, a bird does sing,
Chirping tales of every fling,
Leaves rustle with a giggling cheer,
What mischief lurks in yonder sphere?

A bear in shades, quite out of place,
Dancing with style, a furry grace,
The canopy laughs, all green and bright,
Witnessing antics from morning to night.

So let us raise a toast up high,
To creatures beneath the vibrant sky,
Where nature's jesters frolic and play,
Comedic moments every day!

In the Folds of Flora

In hidden realms of green and brown,
Worms wear tuxedos, twirling 'round,
Flowers gossip, petals unfurled,
Sharing secrets of this tiny world.

A hedgehog walks with a tip-toe flair,
Donning a jump suit, none might dare,
While ants march in a conga line,
Their tiny feet keeping perfect time.

Mushrooms chatter, they're quite the host,
Baking jokes, they love to boast,
Foliage folds disguise their cheer,
As laughter echoes, far and near.

With every rustle, a mystery blooms,
Tiny giggles inhabit the rooms,
So come along, don't miss the fun,
Nature's circus has just begun!

Voices of the Ancient Trees

Old oaks whisper tales of glee,
Telling stories from days carefree,
A fox in slippers, sips on stew,
While wise trees chuckle, as if they knew.

Branches stretch, with limbs out wide,
Inviting the sun for a joyful ride,
In every shadow, laughter rings,
Nature's chorus of silly things.

The willows sway in a dandy dance,
Raccoons in tuxedos, quite the chance,
To join the revelry of this green scene,
Where jesters of the woods roam unseen.

So lend an ear to the ancient beech,
Its leafy wisdom, it longs to teach,
In roots entwined, let laughter be,
The joyful song of the leafy spree!

Oaths Under the Foliage

In a nook where shadows play,
Laughter hums the day away,
A chipmunk vows with pomp and flair,
To become the town's best hair.

The bumblebee a diplomat,
Seeks nectar for a friendly chat,
Under leaves that can't contain,
The giggles from this playful gain.

Frogs in tuxes, jump with style,
Swapping pranks all the while,
Gathering 'round for a meeting grand,
To draw a joke, a merry band.

With every rustling, a promise is made,
To keep the forest's dance parade,
So here we laugh, in fun make claim,
Under foliage, nothing's the same!

www.ingramcontent.com/pod-product-compliance
Lightning Source LLC
Chambersburg PA
CBHW071839160426
43209CB00003B/352